AF484678

Hand
By Antony & Alina Basta

Once upon a time, there was a contest.
Five little fingers debated who's best.

They used to get along, but they each wanted to win.
So they each came up with their reasons, let's listen in...

"I'm the best finger because I can hold many things...

...like pencils, rocks, yarn, and string!"

"No, I'm the best finger because I can point it out."

"There's a train,
there's a car,
there's a boat,
there's a house!"

"No, I'm the best finger
because I can reach really far!"

"If you stand on your toes, I can almost touch the stars!"

"No, I'm the best finger because I'm very special."

"I'm always dressed nice,
with rings of shiny metal."

"No, I'm the best finger because
I'm tiny and small."

"I can reach for things that are stuck between the wall."

"ARGH!"
"UGH!"

POW!!
OUCH!

"WAIT!"

"We all shouldn't fight!
We've been best friends"

"Together we can clap
and count 'til ten."

"We help out one another throughout the day."

"We're all very unique
in our own special way."

With a smile on their face,
the fingers stood fanned

And from that day on,
they lived together as a hand.

THE END.

Dedicated to the Basta and Zeytuntsyan Family

Love, Antony and Alina